Motivated Free Labor Program
Together We Can Make a Difference

Kelly S. Miller

First edition published in March, 2016
First printing March, 2016

ISBN-13: 978-1523959624
ISBN-10: 1523959622

TABLE OF CONTENTS

Background

How did we get here – Many years ago people survived on their own by doing everything for themselves i.e. hunting, gathering, building, cooking, sewing, etc. But at some point as people moved closer together, they found it was easier to focus their efforts in areas they were most successful in, such as hunting. They learned that they could barter their goods or services for others goods and services and this capitalized on everyone's time and efforts. But as time marched on someone figured out a way to turn metal into pretty coins and started convincing people that these metal coins could determine the value of someone's good or service. This started the chase for coin (aka money) and has both grown and exploited humanity ever since.

America has done an outstanding job in bringing the world closer together through its own appetite for world power and technological advancement. Because of our freedoms to create and learn, we have brought the borders of the world to the tips of our fingers. Although this has improved the lives of millions of people around the globe, it also has allowed countries that don't have America's best interests and ideals in mind, to become super powers and key players on the international stage of world power.

The Motivated Free Labor Program (MFLP) is probably not the first of its kind, but it is the right time to create this organization and change America's future in the new 21st century. The program will create a new manufacturing boom in the States and redefine the number of highly educated youth.

MFLP will create a pool of free labor that will benefit the Federal and local governments, as well as create a new manufacturing workforce to bring back all of those "Made in America" jobs that moved over seas. It is time to stop boosting the wallets of countries that would never have the best interest of America at heart and allow companies in America to maximize their revenue streams dramatically by encouraging them to take advantage of all this free labor.

MFLP will also be laser focused on education for both the youth but also all of the adults involved in the program. It is time for America to once again lead the world in education, and MFLP will maximize this effort by taking away all of the social barriers that restrict so many kids and adults today. Technology explosions occur when education is a priority, as was proven when President Kennedy challenged America to go to the moon. MFLP will ignite those same passions for learning by focusing on the seven liberal arts (Grammar, Rhetoric, Logic, Arithmetic, Geometry, Music, and Astronomy), as well as the full spectrum of the sciences, engineering and mathematics.

In order for MFLP to maximize its impact and success in America, it will be necessary to have a MFLP located in every state. This will allow each site to take advantage of natural resources, but also bring the best of each state into the program to boost its success.

Along with some questions answered in the coming chapters, there is also a very simple business plan included that might be helpful to some as an overview or summary of the MFLP. I hope that you can see all of the potential in this idea and how impactful and positive this program would be to so many American's as well as corporate America and our local and federal governments.

Chapter 1 – Why now, why this?

The gap between the haves' and the have not's is growing extremely fast. So if we don't stop and take a step back and make some fundamental changes, America could face some serious challenges with poverty and crime in the not-so-distant future. If you stop and look around us today you will see tent cities popping up, the homeless lines growing bigger and bigger, and even our educational system on the brink of falling to the very last of the line with all of the most powerful nations. If ever there was a time for America to try something new, this is the time.

Many of us that still read and/or watch the news, can see that both local and federal governments are not able to make bold enough progress in areas that could turn things around. The politics of governing and the power of special interest groups have grid locked the system at every level. And the real tragedy is that many of those groups have great ideas and programs they want to implement, but they keep

everything grid locked trying to get their programs through, that

they are all stopping everything from making significant positive

change in America.

And if the grid lock isn't enough, there is a fear of

boldness in our nation. At one time we built the most amazing

road and railway system in the world, and we even sent a man

to the moon. But those men and woman that stood up and

confronted struggle and overcame it, have seemed to fade back

into the shadows of history. So instead of pushing America

forward, these leaders have stepped back into building their

own empires. Because let's be honest here, why would they

step out and get all the stones thrown at them for being so

bold, when it's easier to stay internally focused on developing

and growing corporations interests.

Let's get the "socialism" name tag out there, and

address it up front. MFLP is not a middle or lower class

program, and it most definitely is not a program of something for nothing. It is a program that creates a system that is a win-win for everyone involved. There is no need for us to continue to blame local and federal governments for our struggles, and there is no need to continue to blame corporate America for our problems. There is a need for us to start looking at ways to embrace all of the changes happening in the world and at home, and be the America we all read about in history books. The America that didn't wait for change to knock on the front door or to let other countries dictate what we can and can't do.

It's time for us all to do something together that will motivate American's, create stronger corporations, and give more resources to our local and federal governments than they have ever had. It is time for us to take the headlines of America's history books and commit to greatness once more. We have all read about the great men and woman that lead us to where we are now, now let's make sure our history tells a tell of when we banded together and created a better America for our children and our children's children.

Chapter 2 – Where do we start?

Motivating companies, local and federal governments – The idea of having a fully capable and motivated labor force that is completely free should draw every single American and non-American company to this program, not to mention this labor force being made available to local and federal governments.

When you read about all of the minimum wage battles going on around the United States right now, and really look at what is at the heart of the problem, these people aren't telling these companies that $15 an hour will solve their problems, they are screaming "the current system isn't working for most American's". If you have had the pleasure of taking any small amount of economics in school, you know that the market (people that consume) are willing to pay a certain price for a certain consumable item. Companies spend a lot of money determining what it costs to manufacture that product and what people are willing to pay. So if you are forced to pay more for manufacturing, then you have to make up for this loss somewhere, and that will either be in reduced labor costs by reducing your labor force or finding ways to purchase cheaper quality supplies to lower the cost of manufacturing. Since people are probably not going to buy a product made inferior with cheap parts, the most likely solution for these companies will be to pay higher wages and reduce their head count.

That scenario is a complete lose-lose for everyone and won't solve the problem, plus most of these companies struggling with this issue have a system put in place to have teenagers working those jobs and not people trying to support families. When you look at it that way you can see that it is really a systematic issue and not a wage issue.

To get this all started, we are going to have to get a conversation going with people, manufactures, and local and federal governments. It will take a hard conversation to motivate all of these groups into to looking at the MFLP, but there are so many stories out there about how the current system is just not cutting it and how America needs a new program. The MFLP won't be the solution for all, in fact it can't be, since the commercial industry must have people consuming their products and paying money. This new system is intended to motivate a smaller group of people that want to focus on a different lifestyle than the pursuit of money. There is nothing wrong or right about either one, but it will take a combination of both to restore America's manufacturing dominance around the world again.

The first plan of action after these conversations happen will be to determine which state should host the first prototype community and the pick a handful of companies to invest in this project. It will be critical to document everything that went into building the community, the manufacturing facility, and all of the amenities provided to the first community. This documentation will be critical in going forward with other states and determining exactly what all of the demands for each community will be. There have been so many communities around the United States that have seen some tremendous struggle and devastation from manufacturing leaving the U.S. and going overseas. It would make sense to review these areas and possibly pick one of them to be the first place for one of these communities. Places like Detroit might be a great place to start. But on the other hand so many people have left these communities to find work and pick themselves back up, maybe in states that have a lower unemployment rate would be ideal, so that the impact to the current paying jobs aren't as heavily impacted.

The next key will be finding the right group of people to lead and participate in the first community. These people must be motivated and inspired to be the pioneers of this program and be ready for bumps in the road, that will turn into giant lessons learned for future communities.

Motivating the people – The general desire or willingness of someone to do something. The reason or reasons one has for acting or behaving in a particular way. When many of us were young we'd run straight home after school or get up early on the weekend, just to have the chance to go play with our friends. We didn't need someone pushing us out the door, we knew that if we could meet up with some friends we could create adventures that would last all day long. That same spirit is alive and well in all of us, but with all of the demands of family and life, we have somehow hidden that motivation and inspiration.

If you are going to inspire and motivate a nation or large group of people, then you have to create a system that's long term, sustainable, and duplicate-able around the nation. To do this you first have to develop a community center that allows people to live, work, learn, play and relax in the same area. You have to pull out those same childhood motivations to do something together that will not only change an individuals' life, but lift a nation that disparately needs a kick in the butt.

Living, learning, and planning together in the same community will ensure there are enough resources available to accomplish all of the demands this community will require to grow and flourish. The size of the community should house 100,000 people, which includes both single and family units, with a maximum bedroom count of three bedrooms (larger families could be evaluated to share connecting apartments). Keeping in mind that people will be at the heart and center of everything that happens in the community.

Each housing unit will be fully furnished with a fully functioning kitchen, living room, bathroom(s), and bedroom(s). Because each community will be designed to support different areas of manufacturing, it will be expected that every need for furnishings, clothing, entertainment, food, hygiene, etc. would be available for all of the communities around the United

States. This will boost quality and ensure all of the communities have a constant supply for future growth and needed updates.

Along with furniture each household will be provided with the latest and greatest technologies, as they will also come from one of the communities that manufacture electronics. Having the latest technologies will allow both adults and children access to new technologies, which promote education and healthier living. This access to technology will provide cutting edge technologies to also be tested in these large communities to get very quick feedback to inventors and success stories to promote with the actual product releases to the general public (yet another benefit of the MFLP).

The food will also be supplied from one of the communities, providing a rich supply of fruits, vegetables and meats. Each community will be encourage to educate their members of the benefits of healthy eating and lifestyle, so a lot of attention will go into eating habits and healthy food consumption. These communities will start a new generation of healthy food consumption based on natural foods, and

promoting a-little-to-no processed food consumption diet.

When your mother told you that you are what you eat, these

communities will show the nation and the world just how

powerful those words can be to a healthier and happier

lifestyle.

And as equally important to the others will be the

access to fitness centers, recreational areas and places that

people will be able to relax and enjoy spending time with each

other or by themselves. Even though these communities will be

very large, the need to create an environment that has that

small town sense of health and relaxation by filling the

communities with these wellness areas, will promote

community and wellness like never before. Health and wellness

are giant contributors to motivation and inspiration. They put

that Old Testament drive in a person to get up and move that

mountain.

Facilities for religion and personal wellbeing will also be available to the community, and each community center will be able to vote for exactly what types they will promote (keeping in mind everyone's vote will be looked at).

To ensure the healthiest living conditions possible, the communities will be smoking, alcohol and drug free. There are far too many studies out there that say all of these things are seriously bad for your health, community and families. Each community will put together a group of people that will continually promote these things not being allowed in the community, through education and 100% interaction with everyone. It is probably realistic to understand that some of these things will get into the communities, but if the goal of 100% compliance will keep the bar set high and the offenders will have the opportunity to seek help to quit or be asked to leave the community.

The pinnacle of each community will be the focus on education. Every community will have top notch learning facilities for children, adults and plenty of areas for research and development. Access to both paper and electronic teaching technologies will be provided to everyone in the community. And each community will have a responsibility to provide lessons learned to each of the other communities, ensuring everyone takes advantage of and receives the very best education possible. Outside teachers will be asked to help with educational development, so that after a year or two the communities will be able to provide their own teachers and learning structures.

Finally the manufacturing, agriculture and any other areas of work that will be available to the community will be the very best. They will be designed and constructed by the companies that expect their products and services to be manufactured and sold out of these communities. The quality, speed and quantity of stuff coming out of these communities will be a direct result of both the investment and training provided from the client.

Because everything the community and client need are all provided to the community, the members will have the highest level of motivation possible. These communities will be self-sustaining and not operate with any attachment or need for money, and this will provide a long lasting Motivated Free Labor.

Chapter 3 – Who will do the work?

Labor costs, labor costs, labor costs, those words fill the TV airways day and night and the fight to provide the lowest hourly wages around the world have resulted in some of the most dangerous and inhumane working conditions possible. Not only have the working conditions deteriorated around the world, but the products and services have also suffered. The demand for products and services at bottom line labor prices have accelerated the demand and growth of countries that don't agree or support a free and equal trade civilization, and corruption and control remain king in these new manufacturing cultures around the globe.

So instead of looking at forcing these countries to change or trying to find other countries that will provide even lower hourly wages and support a better national society, America needs to look within and empower people back to manufacturing.

Both commercial and federal manufactures have a demand for low labor costs, which sets the stage for a motivated local workforce that will add more value and dedication to a product and/or services in a time when quality and pride of work is fading away. Asking all of these entities to invest in the MFLP, pool their resources and build and invest in these communities, will result in a manufacturing work force with zero labor costs. Involving the local and federal governments will gain resources for them as well as an opportunity to create tax incentives for the commercial entities to potentially write off the up-front investments to boost American manufacturing.

So now you have facilities built, manufacturing and services ready to be worked and a workforce that has an overwhelming motivation to work and increase their standards of living. The next step is to ensure that the highest quality products are produced; each of the investing entities must ensure they put in place the very best training and best practices for each community, ensuring quality products,

without adding any additional labor costs.

Consistency and quality will be key to the success of
each community, regardless of the product output. To foster
this environment the working day will be held to a 6 hour work
day. With a shorter work day, each person will provide a
stronger focus to their efforts and have a better balance with
their family and community demands. Shorter working days will
also allow for 4 shifts to operate 24 hours a day Vs. 3 shifts of 8
hour each. Rotating shifts will also be easier for people with a 6
hour day.

Because of the amount of people in each community,
there will need to be a certain number of people that will be
motivated to help with the education, food, community
maintenance, and leadership of each community. The
communities could decide if they will rotate or vote in these

roles if they like, but the important thing will be that everyone is involved and agrees to people that fill all of these roles.

Chapter 4 – What could the work be?

The available options for work that will be done in each community center is endless. But we can start off with the basics and expand it from there. The ideal breakdown will be 10% federal government work, 10% local government work and 80% commercial work mixed with all of the necessary functions required to run and maintain each community all for the price of free labor.

If we look at all of the federal government work that these communities could take over and provide for free, you can imagine that federal law enforcement, public community and park maintenance, federal local workers for tax or government ran program purposes. Both fulltime and National Guard units could be housed in these communities. There could even be a federal office area built onto the community that could service the needs of the general public outside of the community.

For local government jobs, the demand for this type of program has never been so desperately needed. There is a large up-front expense for the building of these communities, but the long term payoff in free labor will help every state out tremendously. There are so many local government jobs that could be replaced by the MFLP and free up money for other areas that desperately need the money.

One area that is the MFLP could help is with America's horrible infrastructure. Our roads, bridges, railways and infrastructure could use a free labor force of motivated individuals ready to replace and enhance our infrastructure now and into the future. Plans for speed trains, solar roadways, and all of the technologies needed for America to move into the 21st century, can all finally become a realization and move forward. Getting green technology built and put into place could be a top priority for the MFLP, as well as helping to create badly needed programs to put solar panels on everyone's homes for free, or installing mini windmills in everyone's backyards. The only limit will be how fast the MFLP communities can be built and

planning for all this put into place.

There are many local government jobs that could be

taken over by one of these communities, including police, fire,

local government program workers, etc.

Finally the commercial industry will have the biggest

impact from the MFLP. So much manufacturing has moved

overseas and could be brought back almost overnight as these

communities are built, many will be directly funded from large

corporations ready and excited for this new structure for having

their goods and services produced or provided for free. Almost

everything bought today says made in "somewhere else" and

it's time to bring all of that back to America.

Everything doesn't have to be manufacturing, there

could be giant call centers built or agriculture facilities, or even

services for the elderly outside of these community centers.

Really the only limit will be the imaginations of those companies willing to invest in this idea and see their profit margins go through the roof.

No more spending time and resources paying people to build your products, or wasted time transporting things over in large cargo ships. Instead corporations will be able to fill all those empty cargo containers sitting around America with "made in America" products and send them back to other countries for sale. America would see another great manufacturing boom and all of this will be because both corporate America and motivated American's have a mutually beneficial plan.

Let's talk about product prices a little bit here. Everyone knows the effect Walmart has had on America, both the consumer and many manufactures around the world have benefited. So what if all of that manufacturing moved back to the United States and into these MFL communities? Retailers would have better quality products without the added expenses of labor pushing the margins and forcing the consumer to pay more for less. Retailers could model their distribution and lower

sale prices like Walmart has done and send their products

around the world. On top of labor cost savings, here in the

United States retailers won't have the added expense of

covering the price of shipping their products across the ocean

and being forced to pay whatever manufacturing costs another

country puts in place.

Chapter 5 – How does education play into this MFLP?

The fact that humans can learn and continue to expand their knowledge base, has set us apart from all other species on this planet. And history has shown over and over again, the nations that promoted the best learning avenues for their people, have risen faster and sustained their existence the longest.

It is very difficult to turn on the news or read a paper, and not hear how America has been slipping further and further down the deteriorating educational slope. The headlines continue to read how expensive education is and not what we are doing to change the system that is obviously failing our kids.

The MFLP communities will start to turn this deteriorating trend around by making sure that education for both the young and older are at the center and a huge priority of every center. The key will be to leverage free education at all levels and work with local, federal and corporate clients to make sure that the learning facilities are state of the art and have a review system in place to continually update.

The second key will be to look at all of the learning systems available around the world and take the best of each to develop a new learning curriculum that will put the youth of these communities ahead of everyone around the world. It will also be very important that the new curriculum have a heavy review process to ensure lessons learned are always reviewed and implemented, so that the program is ever evolving and does not become stagnate.

The third key will be the motivated teachers involved in ensuring the highest level of education is taught to the children and adults. And this motivation will come from people that are driven to teach and not driven to make a dollar, ensuring teaching is being done for all the right reasons all the time.

The working day of the MFLP is only 6 hours to ensure families have plenty of time to assist with their children's learning activities as well as spending time developing their own adult education efforts.

Because education will be one of the main pillars of these communities, they will each decide what the appropriate amount of time is required for education. Each community could decide that kids should spend 15 hours a day with a mix of education, exercise and community support, or they could decide that only 8 hours a day is required to meet all of these demands. As communities are established in each state, they will be able to share all of the best practices with each other and together will be able to develop the best program for education.

One of the biggest tragedies we face in America is with continued adult education. The price to continue your education is out of control and more and more adults are not going to continue their education because they can't afford the burden of a mountain of high student loan debt. Just think about all those people that could have the cure for cancer or some new invention that will better humanity forever, but will never be realized because they didn't learn enough through continued education to inspire them to create these.

Continued education for adults will also be free in these communities and will be made available to everyone that is inspired to learn. Each community will house laboratories for learning and technology that will allow them to collaborate with other communities, but also utilize outside college resources made available to them. There could possibly be tax incentives for universities put in place to encourage this knowledge sharing and/or professor volunteering time in teaching at these community centers.

There are so many ways that these communities could research and implement the best educational practices, but the bottom line will be that each community will be required to learn and develop education to its fullest potential and share this knowledge with each community. Their goal will be to set a new high standard for learning at all levels, and continue to evolve it so it only gets better with time.

As these communities develop a robust, results driven educational system, local governments could learn and duplicate this program out into the general public educational system. It might even be a good idea to build a general public education center near one of the MFL communities and have the MFLP provide the program and teachers for this center. This way the general public would also benefit from the best educational system possible, and could possibly help fund further educational program development through low tuition.

Education has to be at the center of every decision this country makes to move us into the 21st century. Without it, America really does face an extremely high mountain to climb to not only catch up, but to get back on top.

Chapter 6 – What will the living conditions be like?

We are born with so many dreams and desires for all of the things in this world and as we get older most find that those dreams start to fade away as we discover financial, educational, social, religious, and many other limiting factors. We start to learn to settle for what is within grabbing distance and most are forced to let those dreams and aspirations fade so that they don't develop symptoms of depression or regret.

The MFLP will create living centers that will provide all of the living essentials necessary for families and individuals to not have to worry about living conditions, clothing, food, learning and recreational needs, and the availability of exercise, spiritual and social centers and other areas that will be used for relaxation and peace of mind. This added benefit from these communities will provide a wealth of benefit to people inside the communities, but also provide the added benefit of reminding how powerful people working towards a common goal, can move beyond individual goals.

After the pilot community has had a little time to get through most of its learning opportunities, the strategy will be to encourage many communities to be built at the same time, so that once complete the manufacturing of goods and services will provide not only for corporate sponsors, but also provide all of the amenities, food, and clothing that will be required by each community.

There will be one to three bedroom apartments made available to each person and family. As more manufacturing of things like clothing, furniture, electronics, food, move back to America, all of these things will also be made available to communities. In the beginning all of this will need to be made available by local and federal governments, as well as corporate sponsors. But once many communities are in full production, then new communities will gain more options to replace or update as needed.

Again the strategy here will be to put in place a group of leaders, organized by the community that will oversee both the current and future needs of the communities, ensuring that everyone has the best living conditions possible and all of their needs are met. To ensure the best results for all of the communities the leadership teams must be rotated to ensure that no special interests distract the communities from having the best possible living conditions.

The architects that work on the design of each community must develop the apartments and facilities for future technology growth. They will need to make sure the latest technology is put in place and keep methods of updating each apartment and community areas are in place. Every community will not be an isolated center, it will be very important that they stay connected to the communities around them. But it will vital to have every effort made to make the communities as self-reliant as possible, through use of solar, wind, and thermal power technologies.

The communities will do everything they can to be self-sufficient including putting in place their own maintenance group. They will ensure that the needs of the community are met and ensure that the utmost level of safety and security is in place. They will ensure the latest fire and natural disaster prevention is in place, along with clear processes of evacuation are in place and practiced by everyone living in the community.

To aid in the burden of local government and community needs, each MFLP community could provide fire, police, and emergency services free of charge. This would ensure that best services are in place and being provided for emergency issues and enhance the level of comfort for all those living in and around the community center.

The location of each community center will also be critical to the success of the community but also to the standard of living in each community. Products and services being offered by each center will need to be close enough to highways and communities that take advantage of the free services, but they also need to be built in areas that allow for visual simulation.

Visual exterior stimulation helps make people feel happy and

providing this stimulation will promote better attitudes and

higher levels of production. The location of the community

should be looked at from an engineering point of view as well,

so that all of the natural energy sources can be used to provide

power, water and possible farming space.

Chapter 7 – What about religion?

Every center will be built with a building intended to support everyone's religious needs. Members from each community will be able to organize their own activities and use the community as they see fit, keeping in mind that the building is intended for all religions.

No matter what faith or background, each center will support and promote all types of spiritual backgrounds. Tolerance and learning from each other will be a key success indicator within the community and should be looked at as a learning example for everyone outside of the MFLP.

Each center will manage how advertising is handled, including if missionaries are allowed to spread their teachings or if the only advertising will be within the religious center. Respecting everyone's choice to worship or not worship and to who or what is very important to people, and the communities will need to basically write the book on how to be truly tolerant and be respectful to others and their beliefs.

Chapter 8 – What about military personnel?

Our great nation was built and defended by some of the most courageous men and woman in history. But the fact remains that many of these men and woman defend our nation and find themselves worrying about money, housing, education, and many other expenses. The MFLP will be a very big supporter of our military community, so that these brave men and woman will have a place to call home and community to come back to. There will be plenty of opportunities for them to contribute to the efforts of the community while they are home and when they are away the community will be there to watch over and ensure their families are taken care of.

As these military personnel are trained to be doctors, engineers, etc., their skills can directly help out the community center. And for those that joined to be solders, well their discipline and hard work ethics will be vital to helping the workforce in the communities perform successfully. When you put the motivation of the community and the discipline gained

from the military, well you create something very special, and

this will ensure the success of every community.

Some of these conflicts around the globe don't seem to

be getting better, and the MFLP will be a great program for

returning solders. They will have the time they need to get

reestablished back into society. They will have all the time they

need for rehabilitation, along with an ideal environment to both

contribute to the manufacturing and community demands, but

also the time to spend getting back into their own family circles,

or even starting a new family within the community.

Chapter 9 – How will people get involved?

Once the community center locations are determined in each state, then a recruiting effort will be started in each state to find leaders in the community that want to participate in this new program and help lead the efforts in their state. Once this process is complete, then they would be teamed up with local and federal workers to start a campaign to find the remaining people and families that what to participate in the program.

Construction of these large community centers will most likely take at least a year, so there will be plenty of time to do interviews and start the process of assimilation into the community center.

People will need to determine if their current possessions will be given to their friends or family members that won't be participating or if they will donate or sale them. They will be provided with clothing, furniture and everything else they need to live very comfortable lives in the community, so there wouldn't be a need to bring anything besides personal memory type objects.

If the person or families have debt, then those debts would be totaled and a new federal program would be set up to pay off those debts. Then as they worked and helped contribute to the community center, those debts would be forgiven. Or in the case that they decided down the road that they wanted to assimilate out of the community and back to their old lives, they would be required to pay off the remaining debts owed to the government.

In the event that people did decide to leave the community, the same local and federal government organization would help them reverse the process and help them get established back into the communities they originated from.

Chapter 10 – A day in the life....

Johnny awoke at his usual time feeling extremely rested and ready for the day. He knew his wife and kids would be sleeping in just a little longer, so he crept into the kitchen to make them a nutritional breakfast. As he entered the kitchen he noticed that there was a green light on in the pantry notifying him that there was a package waiting for him in the drop off area. There were actually three boxes waiting for him; one with fresh groceries, one with new linens and clothing, and the third box had some other miscellaneous items he ordered for his wife and kids as an Easter surprise.

After breakfast Johnny and his wife helped review some study material with their kids and talked about their plans to go on a nature walk later that day to get in some exercise and fresh air. The kids loved going on hikes or doing anything outdoors, since they could always turn these into adventures to share with their classmates the next day.

Johnny and his wife finished getting everyone ready for the day and headed to the elevator, which would take them down to school and even further down to the plant where they spent their 6 hour working day assembling electronics. Johnny and his wife loved working with their hands and enjoyed working together even more.

At the end of their shift in the factory they both volunteered for different groups in the community. Johnny had a passion for the community leadership and would volunteer whenever possible to join committees involved with the growth and future of the center. His wife Julie, on the other hand loved to teach and she would spend 4 or 5 hours every day backfilling any open teaching spots or tutoring children or adults in science and math.

School for their children was 12 hours long each day. This included 8 hours of direct class work, 2 hours of the arts, dance and music, and 2 hour of exercise and fun. The children were allowed to vote on how their 12 hour day would be broke up each quarter. Which ensured the children's dedication to the success of the program, and allowed their schedules to change and not feel stagnant.

At the end of the each day Johnny and his wife would pick up their kids and spend a few hours focused on family fun, learning or spiritual work. They made sure to eat breakfast and dinner together as much as possible and to spend as much time as a family together each day.

It had been a couple years since Johnny and Julie had their old lives, where they felt like everything they were doing was pulling their family in every direction but together. When they read about the MFLP they jumped at the chance to make a huge change, sell everything, and take back control of their family's wellbeing and future. And every day before they go to bed at night, Johnny and Julie pinch each other softly and thank each other for making the decision to be a part of the MFLP.

The Conclusion...

Over the history of America, many have worked for themselves, for small businesses and very large corporations, and it seems most feel the same way. The American dream got manipulated into some dollar chasing race that only a hand full of people are winning. It is the time here and now to try something new, something very far outside the box, and something that allows everyone to win.

You might think that this will destroy the work force or take away paying jobs, and the answer to that is that even if you built a few of these in every state, there will still be millions of people that want to earn a paycheck and not be whiling to give up their current lifestyle.

For those that are tired of chasing the dollar and want to make a bigger impact in their own lives and the future of America, then the MFLP can be that answer. When you read history books, they are full of examples of people that banded together and made different choices and stood up for their

rights to manage their own time. These people changed history

and pushed humanity into better futures with more promise of

education and happiness.

The future of America and promise of a greater

tomorrow can be realized, when we don't spend any more time

worrying about how we will pay for our next meal or how we

will pay for our children or our own educations. When we can

put in a motivated 6 hour day and then come home to spend

quality time with our families or in pursuit of knowledge and

happiness. Personal growth and stronger family ties will be the

back bone of these communities. And with all of that energy,

America will once again become the country of scientific

explosions and breakthroughs. We will become the great

manufacturer of the world again, and we produce goods and

services that are of the highest quality anywhere in the world.

We were once challenged to go to the moon and

beyond, and the MFLP will be the catalyst to this dream

becoming a permanent reality, not something we read in history books. It is time for us to challenge our leaders to make decisions that will help everyone, not just special interest groups.

The hope is this idea resonated with you and it becomes something you could stand behind and support by spreading the message and/or sharing this book.

MFLP (very simple example) Business Plan

Overview

The Community – In each state there would be built a large community center that would house 100,000 people and their families. There would be exercise rooms throughout to promote exercise and a healthier living. A medical center to aid families and provide healthcare needs for the community. Each person and their family would be provided an apartment with up-to 3 rooms and all of the furnishings. Furniture, food, clothing and entertainment needs would also be provided, and each community could leverage their manufacturing surplus to provide for all of the other communities. This would help make them more self-contained.

Manufacturing – Everyone in the community will have a rotational schedule, where they are required to work 6 hours a day. The manufacturing plants will support 24 hour schedules and maximize the six hour shifts. Each community would have a large manufacturing structure attached, and these would be built to take advantage of geological resources. The workforce would be divided up into 10% federal government jobs, 10% local government jobs and 80% commercial jobs. The goal would be to have all of the work done within the manufacturing site, but if resources were needed else were then transportation to and from could be made available.

Education – It will be the responsibility of these communities to continually evolve their educational standards to maximize the results from all of the children and adults participating in it. Each community will be provided the latest technologies and successful teaching practices. Children and adults continuing their education will make it a top priority to learn and take advantage of all of these provided resources. Research labs, community art shows and programs, public discussions and every possible program will be reviewed and made available to each community to promote education throughout the community. Public and private universities will be encouraged to become partners with these communities to encourage collaboration and help drive research in areas that will boost America's technological dominance in the world, and promote discoveries that help enhance life on Earth.

Public to Program Transition – Once the communities are being built and the manufacturing plans for each site are confirmed, then a massive recruiting will take place in each state. People that are excited about participating will be assigned a representative that will aid them in the transition from public life over to the community program. They will need to sell all of their current assets and will be able to move those into a private account or donate money to their family or friends that are not participating in the program. If anyone decided to leave the program, then their representative would assist them back into public life and reverse the process.

Funding – As the communities labor efforts will be divided into 10% Federal, 10% local Government and 80% commercial, so will be the funding requirements for each community. This is why it will be critical to gain all of the support up front. The initial construction costs would be high, but then all of the maintenance and resource needs of each community could be organized and planned in a way that communities were supporting each other and supplying everything internally.

Vision

Five years from now, the MFLP will have started the new manufacturing boom right here in America, and will have proudly put the "Made in America" back on everything produced from American companies. The shift to bring manufacturing to the MFLP from companies outside of America will drive the program to continue to grow and be even more successful.

There will be thousands of children in this program that will take their advancements in education to the next level, and will be leading the world in academic testing and advancement. Because of the advancements in the quality of education, new technologies and scientific breakthroughs will happen effortlessly and consistently on a daily basis.

Mission

The MFLP focuses on providing a new quality of life for all those involved, so that they can focus on providing free quality labor and developing advanced educations. The MFLP Brings people together into communities that provide a support system unparalleled in America today, and accelerates the success of each individual.

Values

Responsibility – America wrote the book on freedom, fairness and doing your part to ensure the success of your family, your state and your country. Somewhere we allowed other countries to take control of our responsibility to our citizens. The MFLP will bring all of those jobs back home to America in a way that will be a win-win for all Americans.

Community – Technology has been driving an isolation wedge in-between everyone in the world, especially here in America. The MFLP will bring thousands of Americans together into tight communities that are dedicated to each other's success and the success of America.

Balance – Americans spend most of their day earning a living and almost no time making a life for themselves and their families. The MFLP will balance the demands for labor with the fulfillment of having a person's housing, clothing, food, education, entertainment and other needs met up-front.

Teamwork – It takes a village! Those words are talked about by many but practiced by few. In order for the MFLP to be a success, every individual involved will need to completely understand how they fit into the big picture and what their impact has on the community. Teamwork will be one of the cornerstones of the MFLP, and will define its success.

Loyalty – The community and ideas will be put into place, but none of that will matter if each individual isn't totally loyal to the vision and mission of the MFLP. Loyalty is contagious and once everyone catches that bug, the communities will be unstoppable and extremely successful.

Farness – The greatest tool the MFLP can leverage will be the community. Nobody will want to do the same job or be in the same role, so to fair to everyone, the community can leverage its numbers to make every job and role either rotatable or interchangeable.

Communications – The idea behind the MFLP is to create communities of 100,000 people living, working, playing and growing together. To make this all work correctly communication will be extremely important and will also be a cornerstone for the MFLP.

Growth – Once the vision is shared, committed to and manufacturing is moved back to America and into the MFLP, the program will explode. This amazing growth will need to be anticipated and planned for ahead of time to ensure the growth is manageable and sustainable.

Trustworthy – Everyone that decides to go into the MFLP will need to know that both the federal and local governments, as well as all of the commercial business, have good intentions and can be trustworthy. Moving into the program will require one to give up their standard way of earning a living and to move into a new community where everyone's efforts will equal success. Trust will defiantly be key to everyone's success.

Quality – Where is the quality? The word quality walked right out of the door with manufacturing that moved to other countries. The MFLP will allow companies to increase the quality of their products since they will be saving money on zero labor costs. "Made in America" will be the quality stamp everyone in America wants to see and will bring a huge sense of pride in the MFLP.

Championing the Cause

In order for the MFLP to grow from an idea into a manufacturing and educational force for the betterment of America, there are four key groups that will need to champion the cause. The plan will be to divide the motivated free labor up into 10% federal support, 10% local government support and then 80% commercial support.

The first group will be at the Federal level and will need bipartisan support from congress. It is extremely important that when discussions start that they are handled with the utmost secrecy to protect America's current manufacturing interests around the world. It will also be important for the federal government to help align all of the communications with the local state government officials as well as assist with identifying corporate sponsors in the manufacturing industry.

The next group that will need to support the MFLP will be at each state level and again bipartisan support will be required to ensure success. It will also be extremely important that communications be held in secrecy so as to not excite the media into false reporting or anything that could delay or deter these efforts.

The third group will be the commercial manufacturing industry. Since they have the most to gain from a motivated free labor workforce, it will be critical to review which states would be most ideal for manufacturing resources and shipping. There will need to be a very detailed plan laid out for each manufacturing company in order to bring up manufacturing in the US and stop manufacturing in other countries.

The last group that will be communicated to will be the very people that will joining the program and changing their lifestyles for this new program and helping change Americas manufacturing system for the new 21st century. They will be impacted the most, since they will need to change their wage mentality focus to a new community focused future. There will need to be a big communication plan put in place for each state, so that each program will gain the most participants.

Objectives and Priorities This Year

The main priority this year will be to make contact with federal government representatives and present the MFLP to them and gain support. Gaining their support and guidance will help drive putting the right people in place and taking the next steps to make the MFLP a reality.

Risks and Opportunities

There are some major risks to the program, the first one being that the idea will not be received and misunderstandings could occur. The project could create so many benefits to America, that if those were not communicated properly they could be swept under the carpet and/or ignored all together.

The next potential risk would be that support will be gained at the federal level, but then at the local state government level support will not be found. Again there will be so many benefits at the local state level, but if local officials do not understand or get the vision of the project, there is risk of rejections.

Another big risk is that the details of this project could leak out to leaders of other countries and they could take steps to damage our current overseas relationships. Many countries have gone from areas of fields to giant high rise landscapes because of all the manufacturing that has moved from America to overseas. Making sure this new project has been successfully put into place before any information is shared with other countries will help lessen the impact to America.

The biggest risk to this project would be that the American public rejected the idea and people were not willing to participate in the program. If there are not enough people to support the manufacturing demands, then the entire program could be at jeopardy as commercial businesses wouldn't want to take the risk of moving their productions back to America.

Another problem that could occur would be that the project was adopted early and the right people weren't put into place to ensure everything is built and put into place correctly. As any vision moves from conception to paper, it is extremely critical for the right people to get put into place to make the vision a successful reality.

When it comes to opportunities there are really countless. If we just look at the numbers, we are looking at each community offering motivated free labor to support 10,000 federal jobs, 10,000 local state jobs and 80,000 commercial jobs at each community. Those number will have an immediate boost to the bottom line of everyone involved and could really help our federal and local governments with resources they desperately need right now. And these numbers would be ideal size community found in each state, so you can really start seeing the power of this project.

When we talk about the opportunities the project offers members of the community it gets even better. Imagine you are currently over worked and still only making ends meet, or most likely not. You have an opportunity to sell all of your possessions and tuck that money away into a safe account or donate it to other family members that don't want to participate in the program, and then move your immediate family into a community center of 100,000 people. You will be given your own apartment with all of the furnishings, along with clothing, food and all the necessities your family requires. Then you have access to a new private educational system for you and your family, along with all the supplies you need for that. There will be areas for exercise and entertainment as well as medical needs provided to you and your family. There will be plenty of job opportunities for you to pick from, and when you learn your work day is on six hours long, you are extremely excited to do whatever you can to make this new project a success.

So internally the community will thrive, but how does that affect the community outside of program. The answer is it will first generate a whole lot of opportunity for jobs in the public sector, since so many will be leaving their public jobs to live and work in the MFLP. This will drive unemployment down in each state and will create public jobs to help build and potentially support these new community centers in their areas.

SWOT Analysis

Strengths:

- The MFLP will redefine and create the next manufacturing boom in America
- People participating in the program will redefine an American citizens contribution to the success of America
- The educational system, research and discovery, and new technologies will keep America in the forefront of the world. And ensure that new modern technologies

and scientific breakthroughs will come from America

efforts.

Weaknesses:

-   The success of the program is dependent on the federal

    government, local governments, the participating

    commercial businesses and the participating workers.

Opportunities:

-   Moving all of Americas manufacturing back to American

    soil could reduce the power and influence of countries

    that don't have America's best interest at heart.

-   Manufacturing, scientific, social, and educational

    breakthroughs could change how everyone in the world

    lives and contributes to the world community.

Threats:

-   The transition of people moving to this new program

    and the availability of people in the public sector to

back fill jobs will need precise focus or some businesses could feel the impact.

- The community will soli be dependent on the resources provided to them.

Management Plan

This business plan will act as a starting point to help deliver the idea, but the blueprints will have many variables that will need to be addressed as each community is planned. A committee should be put into place to oversee the entire project, and as each states community comes online they can develop their own committee to act as a subcommittee to the project.

As each community comes online there will be many opportunities for review and lessons learned, and the main overseeing committee will need to review the project plans regularly.

The Action Plan

This program has so much potential to change the future of America, but as you know our world is filled with many ideas that never come to fruition. The hope is that this book will both start a conversation with big industry and our local and federal leaders, to start looking at other ways to make our great country the greatest country in the world again.

There are many details in this book that would require more time to develop, to ensure the best possible outcomes, but this book should spark some good conversations and set forth a plan to do so much good in America. As a fell American, if you found this books ambitious ideas great, please promote this book with our leaders and corporate American, and

Together We Can Make a Difference

The Author

Kelly Miller is the proud father of two amazing teenagers, and the husband of an amazing wife. He has an MBA and has spent many years as an Account Manager and IT Project Manager. This book represents his passion to look for new ideas outside of the norm, and his love to share ideas that can make America even better than it already is.

Acknowledgement

So much of the information that bombards all of us daily, truly confuses and distracts us from looking outside the box and finding solutions to big issues that face each of our generations. Thank you for taking time to purchase and read this book! It is people like you that look for solutions to problems we face, that ensure America will continue to thrive and remain the greatest nation in the world!

www.ingramcontent.com/pod-product-compliance
Lightning Source LLC
Chambersburg PA
CBHW060414190526
45169CB00002B/900